We live in a time of uncertainty and insecurity. How can we navigate this confusion? How can we cope with so much change? The *Really?* study guide is a great resource to explore how the Christian message enables us to live with real confidence in the real world.
Tim Chester, Director of Porterbrook Seminary

This is every home group's answer to prayer – and for good reason! Nothing is more important in life than knowing what really matters, and every Christian needs to discover that in the Bible and apply it in everyday life. With well-chosen Bible passages, great questions and application, a valuable leader's guide, and even a free email or eBook supplement for each study – this guide is everything a home group needs! Great for personal use too. I hope every church will benefit from buying good quantities!
Jonathan Lamb, CEO and minister-at-large, Keswick Ministries

A study that reaches into the depths of Scripture bringing nourishment, refreshment and hope. There is a feeling at the end that my confidence has grown. God is real and He will prevail!
Fiona McDonald, Director of National Ministries, Scottish Bible Society

Who doesn't grapple with questions of faith and life? This study guide is excellent for individuals or groups using the Bible to face some of the toughest issues head-on.
Peter Maiden, Operation Mobilisation International Director Emeritus

REALLY?

SEARCHING FOR REALITY IN A CONFUSING WORLD

7 Studies for Individuals
or Small Groups

Elizabeth McQuoid

INTER-VARSITY PRESS
Norton Street, Nottingham NG7 3HR, England
Email: ivp@ivpbooks.com
Website: www.ivpbooks.com

First published 2014

British Library Cataloguing in Publication Data
A catalogue record for this book is available from the British Library.

ISBN: 978-1-78359-158-9

Set in Warnock
Typeset in Great Britain by CRB Associates, Potterhanworth, Lincolnshire
Printed and bound in Great Britain by Ashford Colour Press Ltd, Gosport, Hampshire

Inter-Varsity Press publishes Christian books that are true to the Bible and that communicate the gospel, develop discipleship and strengthen the church for its mission in the world.

Inter-Varsity Press is closely linked with the Universities and Colleges Christian Fellowship, a student movement connecting Christian Unions in universities and colleges throughout Great Britain, and a member movement of the International Fellowship of Evangelical Students. Website: www.uccf.org.uk

Contents

Introduction

The digital revolution has opened up a whole new world of opportunity where we can access information at the click of a button. We book our travel online, we follow world news on a smartphone, and our children even google the answers to their homework! We have more access to knowledge than ever before but, paradoxically, we are still searching for truth. Our hearts long for answers to life's ultimate questions. We still search for a way to make sense of life's ups and downs.

The questions don't stop when we become Christians, but God does offer us a new worldview. He promises that in the person of Jesus Christ there is ultimate reality. Jesus himself is real wisdom, truth, security and hope. And when we become his disciples he shares himself and these gifts with us. We uncover the truth about God, we learn what real wisdom is, we experience what it means to be secure, and we have a sure hope for the future.

Christianity is not a neatly packaged reality which makes sense of everything; it doesn't take away the shadows of suffering and doubt. But it is a new, eternal perspective on the world and a promise that one day the answers will come. In the meantime Jesus offers us himself, a reality that satisfies not only our intellectual curiosity, but also the deepest longings of our hearts. Our relationship with Christ is transformational, shaping our thinking and how we live, giving us a brand new identity and purpose.

Can we know ultimate reality? In a world where confusion is still raging, Jesus Christ alone answers that question.

STUDY INTRODUCTIONS

To help participants get the most out of these studies, there is a free supplement, available by email, ebook and in other formats, that introduces the subject of each study. This includes the passage to be studied and an introductory question designed to help anyone begin to think about the subject of each study and how it affects them. It is also designed to be accessible to those who don't have much time to sit down and prepare. These introductions will enrich your study time, and help you get into the right frame of mind. You can register yourself or your group members at www.ivpbooks.com/extras/really

SESSION 1

SESSION 1

Real truth

▶ INTRODUCTION

Pontius Pilate famously asked Jesus, 'What is truth?' And 2,000 years later we are *still* asking the same question. In many ways the search for truth has become more complicated. With the plethora of competing worldviews and different religions, the increase of knowledge via the Internet, and political correctness demanding credibility for everyone's point of view, it is easy to give up on the search for real truth. And yet the Bible pulsates with the message that in Jesus Christ we find real truth. The Gospel writers keep repeating Jesus' well-worn phrase, 'I tell you the truth.' And if Jesus really is the truth – the truth about who God is – and if he tells us the truth, then we can trust him completely, build our lives on his Word and confidently share him with others.

READ *John 14:1-11*

> [1]'Do not let your hearts be troubled. You believe in God; believe also in me. [2]My Father's house has many rooms; if that were not so, would I have told you that I am going there to prepare a place for you? [3]And if I go and prepare a place for you, I will come back and take you to be with me that you also may be where I am. [4]You know the way to the place where I am going.'
>
> [5]Thomas said to him, 'Lord, we don't know where you are going, so how can we know the way?'
>
> [6]Jesus answered, 'I am the way and the truth and the life. No one comes to the Father except through me. [7]If you really know me, you will know my Father as well. From now on, you do know him and have seen him.'
>
> [8]Philip said, 'Lord, show us the Father and that will be enough for us.'
>
> [9]Jesus answered: 'Don't you know me, Philip, even after I have been among you such a long time? Anyone who has seen me has seen the Father. How can you say, "Show us the Father"? [10]Don't you believe that I am in the Father, and that the Father is in me? The words I say to you I do not speak on my own authority. Rather, it is the Father, living in me, who is doing his work. [11]Believe me when I say that I am in the Father and the Father is in me; or at least believe on the evidence of the works themselves.'

 FOCUS ON THE THEME

1. 'Tolerance' is a popular word in our society. Why does our society's idea of tolerance make it difficult to speak out about the truth claims of Christianity?

⬤ WHAT DOES THE BIBLE SAY?

2. Explain in your own words what Jesus is talking about in verses 1–4.

3. Given this context, what does Jesus mean when he says, 'I am the way and the truth and the life'?

4a. What does Jesus say in verses 7–11 about his relationship with his Father? How does this help us understand what Jesus being 'truth' means?

b. Verse 11 says, 'Believe on the evidence of the works themselves.' How do the miracles of Jesus point to the truth of who he is?

I believe in Christianity as I believe that the sun has risen – not only because I see it, but because by it I see everything else.

(Lewis, 'Is Theology Poetry?', p. 21)

◎ INVESTIGATE FURTHER

5.   Look at Romans 1:18–21, 25. What does Paul say unbelievers have done with God's truth?

6.   What does God's truth do for us? Look up:

- Psalm 43:3

- John 8:32

- James 1:18

Many discover that the Christian faith makes sense of life . . . My conversion related to my perception that Christianity offered a more comprehensive, coherent and compelling account of reality than the atheism I had embraced in my earlier teenage years. It seemed to me to possess a double rationality: Christianity made sense in itself, and it made sense of everything else as well. While fully conceding the inevitable limits of arguments from history, experience and reason, I saw these as convergent pointers to the greater reality of God. They couldn't 'prove' the existence of God with the total certainty some might like, but if the God of the Christian faith possessed the profundity, wonder and sheer glory that the New Testament suggested, there was no doubt that he had a deeply embedded capacity to make sense of the riddles of life.

(McGrath, *Mere Theology*, p. 39)

♥ LIVING IT OUT

7.   What comfort does it give to know that Jesus is 'the truth'?

8.   In John 1 Jesus is described as being 'full of grace and truth'. How can we demonstrate these character qualities when we share the gospel with:

- Our non-Christian spouse?

- Our teenage children?

- Work colleagues?

9.   Discuss ways you could answer non-Christian friends who say:

- 'There are many pathways to God; each person has to find his or her own way.'

- 'The Bible can't claim a monopoly on truth. What about all the knowledge and facts we have learned through scientific research?'

- 'I've got my own personal beliefs about God; truth is what is true for me.'

10. Psalm 26:3 (NIV 1984) says, 'I walk continually in your truth.'
     What practical measures can we take to make sure that is true?

▲ PRAYER TIME

Commit to praying daily for five non-Christian family members or
friends. Pray that they would come to know and understand the truth
about God, and that the Holy Spirit would work in their hearts to bring
them to Christ.

Pray for opportunities to share your faith with boldness, clarity and
graciousness.

● FURTHER STUDY

The Truth does not need defending but it does need presenting clearly.
                              (Sinkinson, *Confident Christianity*, p. 17)

It is not our role to defend the Bible: it has its own authority. But we do
have a responsibility to present the case for Christ clearly. Look through
an apologetics book to help you understand and respond to the popular
objections to Christianity and articulate your faith well. Any one of the
books suggested below would be a good place to start.

Krish Kandiah, *Destiny: What's Life All About?* (Monarch, 2007)
Tim Keller, *The Reason for God: Belief in an Age of Scepticism* (Hodder
      and Stoughton, 2008)
Michael Ots, *What Kind of God? Responding to 10 Popular Accusations*
      (IVP, 2008)
Lee Strobel, *The Case for Faith: A Journalist Investigates the Toughest
      Objections to Christianity* (Zondervan, 2000)
Andrew Wilson, *If God, Then What?* (IVP, 2012)

Real identity

▶ INTRODUCTION

When we introduce ourselves to people, we usually describe ourselves in terms of our relationships: 'I'm Jeremy's wife'; 'I'm Mark's mum.' Or we explain who we are by virtue of what we do: 'I'm a teacher'; 'I'm a lawyer.' But what happens when we're widowed, we get divorced, our children leave home, we are made redundant or we retire – who are we then? Who are we when our roles and relationships change? The Bible says our real identity is not based on what we do or who we look after; it doesn't change with each passing season of life. It is based on our unshakeable union with Jesus Christ.

READ *Romans 8:1-4, 9-17*

¹ *Therefore, there is now no condemnation for those who are in Christ Jesus,* ² *because through Christ Jesus the law of the Spirit who gives life has set you free from the law of sin and death.* ³ *For what the law was powerless to do because it was weakened by the flesh, God did by sending his own Son in the likeness of sinful flesh to be a sin offering. And so he condemned sin in the flesh,* ⁴ *in order that the righteous requirement of the law might be fully met in us, who do not live according to the flesh but according to the Spirit . . .*

⁹ *You, however, are not in the realm of the flesh but are in the realm of the Spirit, if indeed the Spirit of God lives in you. And if anyone does not have the Spirit of Christ, they do not belong to Christ.* ¹⁰ *But if Christ is in you, then even though your body is subject to death because of sin, the Spirit gives life because of righteousness.* ¹¹ *And if the Spirit of him who raised Jesus from the dead is living in you, he who raised Christ from the dead will also give life to your mortal bodies because of his Spirit who lives in you.*

¹² *Therefore, brothers and sisters, we have an obligation – but it is not to the flesh, to live according to it.* ¹³ *For if you live according to the flesh, you will die; but if by the Spirit you put to death the misdeeds of the body, you will live.*

¹⁴ *For those who are led by the Spirit of God are the children of God.* ¹⁵ *The Spirit you received does not make you slaves, so that you live in fear again; rather, the Spirit you received brought about your adoption to sonship. And by him we cry, 'Abba, Father.'* ¹⁶ *The Spirit himself testifies with our spirit that we are God's children.* ¹⁷ *Now if we are children, then we are heirs – heirs of God and co-heirs with Christ, if indeed we share in his sufferings in order that we may also share in his glory.*

FOCUS ON THE THEME

1. Why does the issue of identity matter so much to us?

WHAT DOES THE BIBLE SAY?

2. What phrases does Paul use to describe our identity in verses 12–17?

3. How do we receive this new identity of being 'in Christ' according to verses 1–4?

4. What is the hallmark of our new identity? Look at verses 9–11.

5. Look back over verses 12–17. How does the Holy Spirit help us live out our new identity?

◎ INVESTIGATE FURTHER

6. How does Peter describe the church's identity in 1 Peter 2:4–5, 9? What do these images convey about the church's role?

7. What difference should our new identity make to how we live? What does Peter say in 1 Peter 2:11–12?

Do I, as a Christian, understand myself? Do I know my own real identity? My own real destiny? I am a child of God. God is my Father; heaven is my home; every day is one day nearer. My Saviour is my brother; every Christian is my brother too. Say it over and over to yourself first thing in the morning, last thing at night, as you wait for the bus, any time when your mind is free, and ask that you may be enabled to live as one who knows it is utterly and completely true. For this is the Christian's secret of – a happy life? – yes, certainly, but we have something both higher and profounder to say. This is the Christian's secret of a Christian life, and of a God-honouring life: and these are the aspects of the situation that really matter. May this secret become fully yours, and fully mine. (Packer, *Knowing God*, p. 256)

♥ LIVING IT OUT

8. Romans 8:14 reminds us that God's children are 'led by the Spirit.' What spiritual practices increase your awareness of the Holy Spirit's leading?

9. What would you say to an unbeliever who claimed you were arrogant for believing you're God's child and your place in heaven is secure?

10. How is your identity as God's child shaped by being part of the church? What difference does it make:

- To be part of a small group?

- To be part of a ministry team?

- To have a small group of friends to pray with?

- To regularly attend worship services?

▲ PRAYER TIME

In the relentless busyness of juggling all our roles and responsibilities it is often difficult to maintain focus on our real identity. Pray for the family, work and church struggles group members are going through. Pray that in each case they would remember their real identity as God's child, they would know the Holy Spirit's leading and please God with their obedience this week.

Worship is so important for Christian identity. It focuses our attention on what really matters, and proclaims that the Christian faith has the power to capture the imagination – not merely to persuade the mind – by throwing open the depths of the human soul to the realities of the gospel.

(McGrath, *Mere Theology*, p. 4)

 **FURTHER STUDY**

Investigate what it means for us to be 'adopted' as God's children – when were we adopted, why, what are our privileges and rights? Look up 'adopted' in a concordance or at www.biblegateway.com. A useful starting point would be Galatians 4:1–7; Ephesians 1:4–6; and 1 John 3:1–2.

Real wisdom

▶ INTRODUCTION

If wisdom was just about acquiring knowledge, our Wikipedia generation would be the wisest there has ever been. If wisdom was simply about gaining experience, we'd all get wiser as we get older. Wisdom includes knowledge and experience but it's more than that; it's hard to quantify but we know it when we see it! The Bible talks a lot about wisdom – the Psalms and Proverbs are full of its teaching; the apostle Paul contrasts worldly and godly wisdom; and Jesus is presented as the pinnacle of wisdom: He 'has become for us wisdom from God – that is, our righteousness, holiness and redemption' (1 Corinthians 1:30). Finding real wisdom is costly, but it is a treasure worth searching for because it teaches us how to live wisely, how to live well in God's sight.

READ *Job 28:12–28*

¹²*But where can wisdom be found?*
Where does understanding dwell?
¹³*No mortal comprehends its worth;*
it cannot be found in the land of the
living.
¹⁴*The deep says, 'It is not in me';*
the sea says, 'It is not with me.'
¹⁵*It cannot be bought with the finest gold,*
nor can its price be weighed out in silver.
¹⁶*It cannot be bought with the gold of Ophir,*
with precious onyx or lapis lazuli.
¹⁷*Neither gold nor crystal can compare with it,*
nor can it be had for jewels of gold.
¹⁸*Coral and jasper are not worthy of mention;*
the price of wisdom is beyond rubies.
¹⁹*The topaz of Cush cannot compare with it;*
it cannot be bought with pure gold.

²⁰*Where then does wisdom come from?*
Where does understanding dwell?
²¹*It is hidden from the eyes of every living thing,*
concealed even from the birds in the sky.
²²*Destruction and Death say,*
'Only a rumour of it has reached our ears.'
²³*God understands the way to it*
and he alone knows where it dwells,
²⁴*for he views the ends of the earth*
and sees everything under the heavens.
²⁵*When he established the force of the wind*
and measured out the waters,
²⁶*when he made a decree for the rain*
and a path for the thunderstorm,
²⁷*then he looked at wisdom and appraised it;*
he confirmed it and tested it.

> ^{28}*And he said to the human race,*
>   *'The fear of the Lord – that is wisdom,*
>   *and to shun evil is understanding.'*

◉ FOCUS ON THE THEME

1. How would you define 'wisdom'? What is the difference between wisdom and knowledge?

Q WHAT DOES THE BIBLE SAY?

2. According to verses 12–22:
    a. Why is the search for wisdom so worthwhile?

    b. Where is wisdom not found?

3. Why is God qualified to know real wisdom (verses 24–27)?

4.   How can we access true wisdom (verse 28)?

Job 28:28 gives divine affirmation to Job (and to us) that we need no secret of the higher life, no mysterious spiritual law to raise us to a deeper level of spirituality or godliness, no 'answers' achieved only by some spiritual elite. No, we are called, as was Job, to begin our lives of discipleship with the fear of God and repentance from evil, and to continue our walk with God exactly the way we started it (cf. Colossians 2:6).

(Ash, *Out of the Storm*, p. 74)

◎ INVESTIGATE FURTHER

5.   Abraham is the first person in the Bible said to 'fear God'. Scan Genesis 22:1–12. What do we learn from this account about what it means to 'fear God'?

6.   What else can we learn about what 'fearing God' means? Look at:

- Psalm 147:11

- Proverbs 8:13

- Isaiah 33:6

7.   Psalm 1 describes the two choices in life – those who follow God's wisdom and those who don't.

a.   According to verses 1–2, what does it mean to live wisely?

b.   What are the results of living according to God's wisdom?

♥ LIVING IT OUT

8.   How can we help our children or new Christians to not just know the facts about God but actually live wisely?

9.   How can focusing on God's wisdom help us when we don't understand the reasons for our suffering or feel God is not being fair?

10.   In what kind of issues or situations do we struggle to submit to God's wisdom? What practical steps can we take to trust him in these areas?

We express our fear of the Lord when we trust him with our circumstances – as uncomfortable or confusing as they may be. We trust him enough to accept that there need not be an explanation. We trust that his just nature is unassailable even though there is no identifiable justice in the circumstances in which we find ourselves. We trust that he has set up the system in the very best (=wisest) way possible even when we are suffering the consequences of a system broken by the fall. We trust his love for us, and we trust that even in our difficulties, he can show his love and strengthen us through the trials.

(Walton, *Job: The New International Commentary*, pp. 300–301)

▲ PRAYER TIME

If it is appropriate, pray about some of the issues you discussed in question 10. Pray for each other that you would model the wisdom described in Psalm 1, that you would be like trees planted with deep roots in God.

I keep asking that the God of our Lord Jesus Christ, the glorious Father, may give you the Spirit of wisdom and revelation, so that you may know him better.
(Ephesians 1:17)

● FURTHER STUDY

Read through the book of Job. Why did Job's friends think he was suffering? What is wrong with their point of view? How does taking account of God's wisdom challenge their perspective?

Real purpose

▶ INTRODUCTION

If you go onto the Amazon website and click on the shopping basket icon, the message pops up: 'Give it purpose – fill it with books, DVDs . . .' The advertisers are reminding us that purpose and value come from doing what we were created for. Right back in Genesis 1 God designed us to be useful and productive, to gain achievement and a sense of purpose from work and caring for others. But God had bigger plans for us, eternal plans; consequently our true purpose is based on something more than earthly accomplishments. The Westminster Confession states: 'Man's chief end is to glorify God, and to enjoy him forever.' When we put God at the centre of our lives and follow him, then we find real purpose because all that we do on earth is invested with eternal significance and value.

READ *Philippians 3:7–14*

⁷*Whatever were gains to me I now consider loss for the sake of Christ.*
⁸*What is more, I consider everything a loss because of the surpassing worth of knowing Christ Jesus my Lord, for whose sake I have lost all things. I consider them garbage, that I may gain Christ* ⁹*and be found in him, not having a righteousness of my own that comes from the law, but that which is through faith in Christ – the righteousness that comes from God on the basis of faith.* ¹⁰*I want to know Christ – yes, to know the power of his resurrection and participation in his sufferings, becoming like him in his death,* ¹¹*and so, somehow, attaining to the resurrection from the dead.*

¹²*Not that I have already obtained all this, or have already arrived at my goal, but I press on to take hold of that for which Christ Jesus took hold of me.* ¹³*Brothers and sisters, I do not consider myself yet to have taken hold of it. But one thing I do: forgetting what is behind and straining towards what is ahead,* ¹⁴*I press on towards the goal to win the prize for which God has called me heavenwards in Christ Jesus.*

FOCUS ON THE THEME

1. What roles or jobs give you a sense of purpose?

WHAT DOES THE BIBLE SAY?

2. Paul says his chief purpose is to 'know Christ'. Looking at verses 7–11, explain what he means by this.

3. Paul says, 'Whatever were gains to me I now consider loss for the sake of Christ.' According to verse 9, what changed his focus? Why has his purpose changed?

4. How does Paul convey his urgency to know Christ in verses 12–14?

It's in Christ that we find out who we are and what we are living for. Long before we first heard of Christ and got our hopes up, he had his eye on us, had designs on us for glorious living, part of the overall purpose he is working out in everything and everyone.

(Ephesians 1:11–12 MSG)

⊙ INVESTIGATE FURTHER

5. Scan Philippians 1:12–27. Paul's purpose is to 'know Christ and make him known'. How does this affect his view of:

    • Suffering (verses 12–14)?

    • Death (verses 20–24)?

    • Ministry (verses 23–27)?

6.   Look up the following verses. What more details do they give us about God's purposes for us?

   *   Ephesians 2:10

   *   2 Timothy 1:9

   *   2 Corinthians 5:18–20

We often embrace the 'shotgun' approach to life, trying to find happiness and satisfaction by scattering our time and energies over a wide range of interests and activities. We want to try a little bit of everything, and we do not want to miss out on anything. Paul suggests we use the 'rifle' approach by finding the single priority that makes life worth living, that is, the Lord Jesus Christ, and give ourselves unreservedly to it.

(Ellsworth, *Opening up Philippians*, p. 67)

♥ LIVING IT OUT

7.   In Philippians 3:13 Paul said he pursued his goal of knowing Christ, 'forgetting what is behind and straining towards what is ahead'. In order to know Christ better:

   *   What things do you need to forget?

   *   What action do you need to take to 'strain towards what is ahead'?

8.   Part of God's purpose is that we share the gospel with others (2 Corinthians 5:20). What ways have you found to do this?

9. 1 Corinthians 10:31 says, 'Whatever you do, do it all for the glory of God.' How can we be more conscious of doing our daily tasks of parenting, going out to work and so forth for God's glory? How can we bring eternal purpose and value to these tasks?

10. Sum up what you think God's purpose is for you.

Scripture tells us that we were created to glorify God, indicating that we are important to God himself. This is the final definition of genuine importance or significance to our lives: If we are truly important to God for all eternity, then what greater measure of importance or significance could we want?

(Grudem, *Systematic Theology*, pp. 440–441)

▲ PRAYER TIME

Meditate on Philippians 3:12: 'I press on to take hold of that for which Christ Jesus took hold of me.' Think back to your conversion when Christ 'took hold of you'. Consider all that he had in mind for you when he saved you. Renew your commitment to 'press on' and daily listen for God's 'upwards call'. Pray for each other in the group that your faith wouldn't stagnate and you'd have renewed passion for 'knowing Christ'.

 FURTHER STUDY

Acts 13:36 states that King David 'served God's purposes in his own generation'. Read about David's life in 1 Samuel 16 – 1 Kings 2:10. You can scan some of these verses; others take time to read more closely. How did David serve God's purposes? What lessons can we apply to our own lives?

SESSION 5

Real security

▶ INTRODUCTION

We crave security – personal safety, control and peace. We go to extraordinary measures to protect ourselves from harm and make ourselves less vulnerable: locks, passwords, bank accounts and so much more. But despite our best efforts there is still so much of life we have no control over; our security is precarious. Christianity offers us security – not physical security but soul security; a peace with God that can weather all the ups and downs of life; an eternal security which starts now.

READ *Psalm 46*

¹*God is our refuge and strength,*
 an ever-present help in trouble.
²*Therefore we will not fear, though the earth give way*
 and the mountains fall into the heart of the sea,
³*though its waters roar and foam*
 and the mountains quake with their surging.

⁴*There is a river whose streams make glad the city of God,*
 the holy place where the Most High dwells.
⁵*God is within her, she will not fall;*
 God will help her at break of day.
⁶*Nations are in uproar, kingdoms fall;*
 he lifts his voice, the earth melts.

⁷*The* LORD *Almighty is with us;*
 the God of Jacob is our fortress.

⁸*Come and see what the* LORD *has done,*
 the desolations he has brought on the earth.
⁹*He makes wars cease*
 to the ends of the earth.
He breaks the bow and shatters the spear;
 he burns the shields with fire.
¹⁰*He says, 'Be still, and know that I am God;*
 I will be exalted among the nations,
 I will be exalted in the earth.'

¹¹*The* LORD *Almighty is with us;*
 the God of Jacob is our fortress.

 ## FOCUS ON THE THEME

1. What do people do to make themselves feel secure?

⬤ WHAT DOES THE BIBLE SAY?

2. What does this psalm say to people who assume life should be easier now they are Christians?

3. Who will not enjoy God's security?

4. What ultimate security does God offer (verse 10)?

⦿ INVESTIGATE FURTHER

5. What else does the Bible say about the security God offers now while we are going through difficulties? Look at:

- Romans 8:28

- Philippians 1:4–6

- Hebrews 4:14–16

6. What does the Bible say about the security of our salvation?
    Look at:

    • John 10:27–30

    • Romans 5:6–11

    • Romans 8:35–39

7. Sometimes our faith is challenged by external factors, but often
    it's our own doubts which cause us to struggle. Look at Psalm 77,
    particularly verses 10–20. What did the psalmist do to renew his
    confidence in God?

*Doubt is often a symptom of a faith that needs to grow – to put down
deeper roots . . . Viewed positively doubt tests your faith, and shows you
where it is vulnerable. It forces you to think about your faith, and not just
take it for granted. It stimulates you to strengthen the foundations of your
relationship with God.* (McGrath, *Doubt in Perspective*, p. 139)

 LIVING IT OUT

8. If it is appropriate, share examples of when:
    a. You have faced doubts or challenges to your faith

b. Confidence in your faith has been renewed

c. The strength of your faith has been a witness to unbelievers

9. What are the main challenges facing the church today? How can the church stand secure?

10. In what ways can you demonstrate that your security is in God alone? In what areas of your life would you have to make practical changes?

God does not love us because we are serviceable; He loves us simply because He loves us. This is the only kind of love we can ever be secure in, of course, since it is the only kind of love we cannot possibly lose. This is grace.

(Keller, *Galatians for You*, p. 30)

PRAYER TIME

Psalm 46:10 reminds us that the security God offers – his protection, help and ultimate victory – often doesn't hit us or impact our lives until we come before him quietly. Take time to be quiet before God; meditate on his character and all that he has done for you. Pray for each other that you would recognize the false security the world offers and trust in God alone.

 FURTHER STUDY

If you would like to investigate more about how to deal with doubt and the confidence we can have in Christ, the book *Doubt in Perspective* by Alister McGrath is an excellent resource.

Real treasure

▶ INTRODUCTION

Did you ever dig for treasure as a child? For those of us who still enjoy treasure hunts, the British Treasure Act of 1996 stipulates what constitutes treasure and what to do if you find it! The joy of searching and finding treasure shouldn't surprise us; we were designed for it. God made us with a sense of curiosity and a desire to search for something better. Life is filled with many distractions that glisten like treasure but, ultimately, only Christ satisfies. He is a treasure of immeasurable worth, one we will have to search for and sacrifice everything for but that will change our lives forever. The Bible describes Christ's rule in our lives as the 'kingdom of heaven' and says it is worth letting go of everything else to enter it. As the missionary Jim Elliot said, 'He is no fool who gives what he cannot keep to gain that which he cannot lose' (Elliot, *In the Shadow of the Almighty*, p. 108).

READ *Matthew 13:44–46*

⁴⁴The kingdom of heaven is like treasure hidden in a field. When a man found it, he hid it again, and then in his joy went and sold all he had and bought that field.

⁴⁵Again, the kingdom of heaven is like a merchant looking for fine pearls. ⁴⁶When he found one of great value, he went away and sold everything he had and bought it.

 ## FOCUS ON THE THEME

1. What would your friends say you treasure most?

 ## WHAT DOES THE BIBLE SAY?

2. Describe the different ways these two people found the kingdom of heaven. How does this reflect the different ways people become Christians?

3. How do these two people who found the kingdom of heaven differ? How is this like the variety of people who become Christians?

4. What is the shared theme of these two parables?

The kingdom of heaven is of supreme value. When we find it ('fully grasp its infinite worth'), we will joyfully let go of all competing claims on our lives and make it our one great possession.

(Mounce, *New International Biblical Commentary: Matthew*, p. 135)

◉ INVESTIGATE FURTHER

5. What kind of sacrifice is involved in finding real treasure? Look at:
   - Matthew 19:16–21

   - John 12:23–26

   - 1 Timothy 6:17–19

6. According to Matthew 19:29–30, what is promised to those who make this kind of sacrifice?

7. According to 2 Corinthians 4:7, what happens when we find real treasure?

And God said to me, 'Instead of asking, "Is it worth it?" and looking at the price you think you have to pay, would you ask, "Am I worthy?"' And as soon as you say, 'Is he worthy?' you realize our amazing privilege – of course he's worthy! There's nothing he brings into our lives or allows to occur in our lives that he is not able to handle and cope with and he's entrusting it to you. A clay jar, easily brittle, easily breakable, often cracked, but indwelt by the most precious treasure, the lovely Lord Jesus ... We are called by God, we are sent out to serve him, we are commissioned, and there will be moments in all our lives when it's tough, it's hard going, and if you ask 'Is it worth it?' you'll be tempted to say, 'No.' But lift up your hearts and your eyes to Jesus, fix your eyes on him as Hebrews tells us, and you'll find that he'll never fail you, he'll never let you down, he is worthy.

(Roseveare, in *Word to the World*, p. 51)

♥ LIVING IT OUT

8.   In Revelation 3:15–16 Christ rebuked the church in Laodicea because it had lost its passion and was becoming lukewarm in its devotion. How can we make sure we 'treasure' Christ in our churches and keep him our main priority?

9.   Mary proved that Jesus was her treasure when she anointed him with expensive perfume (John 12:1–10). What could you give to Christ as an act of extravagant devotion?

- Extra time to help a church project

- Cheerfully using your talents to serve someone else

- A sacrificial gift of money

- Something else?

If Jesus Christ be God and died for me, then no sacrifice can be too great for me to make for him. (C. T. Studd, personal motto)

10. Imagine you are the clay jar in 2 Corinthians 4:7. What difference does it make to remember that the treasure of Christ is in you, shining out to others?

PRAYER TIME

Christ in us is the end of all our searching; the only treasure worth giving up everything for. Yet amazingly, not only is Christ our treasure; we are his. Sometimes we forget how very much God loves us. The Bible tells us we are the apple of God's eye; our names are graven on Christ's hands; we are his joy and delight. Spend time together thanking God for how much he loves you. Ask the Holy Spirit to help you this week treasure Christ and put him first, not out of duty, but in response to how very much we are loved by him.

For you are a people holy to the Lord your God. The Lord your God has chosen you out of all the peoples on the face of the earth to be his people, his treasured possession. (Deuteronomy 7:6)

 FURTHER STUDY

Read a Christian biography and be inspired by those who have made
Christ their treasure whatever the cost. Below are a few suggestions to
help you get started.

Arnold Dallimore, *George Whitefield* (Crossway, 2010)
Elisabeth Elliot, *Through Gates of Splendour: The Five Missionary Martyrs
    of Ecuador* (Authentic, 2006)
Sharon James, *My Heart in His Hands* (Evangelical Press and Services,
    2006) – a biography of Ann Judson, missionary to Burma
Eric Metaxas, *Bonhoeffer: Pastor, Martyr, Prophet, Spy* (Thomas Nelson,
    2010)

Real hope

 INTRODUCTION

'Everything will be all right in the end . . . if it's not all right then it's not yet the end' (Sonny, *The Best Exotic Marigold Hotel*, 2011). Christianity is unique among all the religions of the world because it offers us a sure and certain hope for the future, a home in heaven. But more than that, Jesus Christ offers us hope for each day. As we get to know Jesus through the Bible, he helps us make sense of our struggles and gives us a glimpse of the bigger picture of how God is working in the world.

READ *Romans 8:18-39*

¹⁸*I consider that our present sufferings are not worth comparing with the glory that will be revealed in us.* ¹⁹*For the creation waits in eager expectation for the children of God to be revealed.* ²⁰*For the creation was subjected to frustration, not by its own choice, but by the will of the one who subjected it, in hope* ²¹*that the creation itself will be liberated from its bondage to decay and brought into the freedom and glory of the children of God.*

²²*We know that the whole creation has been groaning as in the pains of childbirth right up to the present time.* ²³*Not only so, but we ourselves, who have the firstfruits of the Spirit, groan inwardly as we wait eagerly for our adoption to sonship, the redemption of our bodies.* ²⁴*For in this hope we were saved. But hope that is seen is no hope at all. Who hopes for what they already have?* ²⁵*But if we hope for what we do not yet have, we wait for it patiently.*

²⁶*In the same way, the Spirit helps us in our weakness. We do not know what we ought to pray for, but the Spirit himself intercedes for us through wordless groans.* ²⁷*And he who searches our hearts knows the mind of the Spirit, because the Spirit intercedes for God's people in accordance with the will of God.*

²⁸*And we know that in all things God works for the good of those who love him, who have been called according to his purpose.* ²⁹*For those God foreknew he also predestined to be conformed to the image of his Son, that he might be the firstborn among many brothers and sisters.* ³⁰*And those he predestined, he also called; those he called, he also justified; those he justified, he also glorified.*

³¹*What, then, shall we say in response to these things? If God is for us, who can be against us?* ³²*He who did not spare his own Son, but gave him up for us all – how will he not also, along with him, graciously give us all things?* ³³*Who will bring any charge against those whom God has chosen? It is God who justifies.* ³⁴*Who then is the one who condemns? No one. Christ Jesus who died – more than that, who was raised to life – is at the right hand of God and is also interceding for us.* ³⁵*Who shall*

separate us from the love of Christ? Shall trouble or hardship or persecution or famine or nakedness or danger or sword? [36]As it is written:

'For your sake we face death all day long;
we are considered as sheep to be slaughtered.'

[37]No, in all these things we are more than conquerors through him who loved us. [38]For I am convinced that neither death nor life, neither angels nor demons, neither the present nor the future, nor any powers, [39]neither height nor depth, nor anything else in all creation, will be able to separate us from the love of God that is in Christ Jesus our Lord.

FOCUS ON THE THEME

1. What are you hoping for? At this point in your life what are your hopes for the future?

WHAT DOES THE BIBLE SAY?

2. According to verses 18–23, what hope do Christians have?

3. What guarantees do we have of this future hope? Look at verses 23, 28–30.

4. What does this hope mean for life now? How does this future hope impact the present? Look at verses 31–39.

In the Bible, hope is not a vague expectation – a kind of fingers-crossed wishful thinking. Rather, it is the Bible's shorthand for unconditional certainty. Hope is a sure and confident expectation about the future, based on a trust in God's sovereignty and a confidence in his faithfulness. True hope is future-orientated and grounded in the character of God and the fact that he has committed himself to us in the form of his unbreakable promises. Hope is therefore the confident anticipation of a future outcome.

(Mallard, *Invest Your Suffering*, p. 166)

⊙ INVESTIGATE FURTHER

5. What is the reason for our future hope given in 1 Peter 1:3–5?

6. Why can we put our hope in God during difficult times? Look at:

    - 1 Peter 1:6–7

    - 2 Corinthians 4:16–18

7. What difference can real hope make to our lives now?
Look up:

- Isaiah 40:31

- 1 Thessalonians 1:3

- Hebrews 6:17–20

- 1 John 3:3

We assume that, in our trials, God has forgotten us or that they prove that we are of no value to him. Precisely the opposite is true. God tests us because we are precious and he wants to remove the dross and prove the reality of our faith. The fire of the furnace is proof of intentional grace and deliberate mercy. (Mallard, *Invest Your Suffering*, pp. 96–97)

 LIVING IT OUT

8. In what ways can we share God's hope with:

- Christian friends going through difficult times?

- Friends who don't share our Christian faith?

- Our local community?

9. Consider your own concerns and struggles. How do these Bible truths

    - challenge you?

    - comfort you?

To be honest, during the last twenty years there have been times when my faith has seemed frail and fragile and almost ready to collapse. But one thing I have never doubted is that, in the darkest circumstances, we were only ever in the hands of God. That has been the ultimate source of comfort and hope. (Mallard, *Invest Your Suffering*, pp. 34–35)

10. Reflect on your answer to question 1. What do you think God wants you to hope for? What practical measures could you take to get your focus right?

My hope is built on nothing less
Than Jesus' blood and righteousness.
I dare not trust the sweetest frame,
But wholly trust in Jesus' Name. (Edward Mote)

▲ PRAYER TIME

- Thank God for being a constant source of hope.
- Pray about the hopes for yourself and your family you mentioned in question 1.
- Ask God to help you keep eternity your real hope and focus.

May the God of hope fill you with all joy and peace as you trust in him, so that you may overflow with hope by the power of the Holy Spirit.

(Romans 15:13)

 ## FURTHER STUDY

Look up the word 'hope' in a concordance or at www.biblegateway.com. Study the Bible references and find out more about the basis for our hope and how having hope can impact our lives now.

Leader's guide

As a leader, your role is not to answer every question but to facilitate group discussion and to help people focus on what God's Word says. Make sure you make time during the week to read the Bible passages and questions. Look at the leader's guide and see how best to present the questions and generate discussion.

If you are to make the most of your group time, it is a great help if each group member can read the passage and think about the subject of the study in advance. Of course, this is difficult when members don't have much time to sit down and prepare. To help with this, there is a short supplementary introduction for each study. You can sign up your group members to receive this in advance each week. It includes the passage to be discussed, as well as something to help the reader begin to think about the subject of the week's study. These introductions are very short, simple and accessible – ideal for busy people. See www.ivpbooks.com/extras/really for a sample.

The supplement is automatically delivered each week to those who have signed up, either as an ebook, email or a PDF which is easily readable or printable. See the website for further details of how to receive it.

Don't rush through the study; feel free to miss some questions out and focus on what's most pertinent to your group. The aim is not just to learn about the issues under discussion but to see how they impact our life and are foundational to our faith.

Be aware of the group dynamics. Some people are eager to contribute and others less so. You may have to encourage quieter folk to participate and ask the more vocal ones to listen! Invite a number of replies to each question so that people share what they have prepared and learn from one another's responses.

It is important to leave time at the end of the session for prayer and to sum up what God has taught you. Make sure the group members go home clear about the main message of the study and how they are going to apply it in their lives in the coming week.

Your group may be well established and your members prepared to talk at a deep level. New groups take time to settle but, as your group members get to know one another, you'll not just be talking about the issues but developing a true sense of Christian community as you pray, share, learn and grow together.

They are not integral to the study, but the 2014 Keswick Convention talks, 'Really?', are available on DVD or CD and can be downloaded free at www.keswickministries.org. Leaders, individuals or your small group could use these to complement the study.

SESSION 1

Real truth

1. Being tolerant is very important in our society. In practice this means a 'live and let live' approach to life where we don't criticize other people's views and they don't criticize ours. We are kind to each other as long as we both agree that whatever we say is true, and every view is right and of equal worth. The exclusive claims of Christianity, what Jesus said about being the only way to God, and the command to share this good news doesn't fit well with this current view of tolerance. However, real tolerance is being kind, loving and patient even when we completely disagree with someone.

2. Jesus is talking about heaven. By his act of dying on the cross and rising again, he is preparing a place for believers to join him there.

3. Jesus is answering Thomas's question: 'We don't know where you are going, so how can we know the way?' So being 'the way' is the main idea in verse 6. Jesus is saying, 'I am the way to God because I am the truth of God and the life of God.'

> *Jesus is the truth, because he embodies the supreme revelation of God – he himself 'narrates' God (1:18), says and does exclusively what the Father gives him to say and do (5:19ff, 8:29), indeed he is properly called 'God' (1:1, 18; 20:28). He is God's gracious self-disclosure, his 'Word', made flesh (1:14). Jesus is the life (1:4), the one who has 'life in himself' (5:26), 'the resurrection and the life' (11:25), 'the true God and eternal life' (1 John 5:20). Only because he is truth and life can Jesus be the way for others to come to God … and therefore the answer to Thomas' question.*
>
> (Carson, *The Gospel According to John*, p. 491)

4a. Jesus explains he is the truth about God because he fully reveals God. If the disciples have seen Jesus they have had a full and true revelation of God. Jesus speaks the Father's words and does his work, so at every level he is communicating God's truth.

4b. The miracles of Jesus and all that they signify point to Jesus being truly God. For example, turning the water into wine was evidence of Jesus' divinity, but the miracle itself was a signpost to Jesus' glory and that he was ushering in the new kingdom, the messianic age people had been waiting for.

5. These are hard words and a difficult passage. Try not to let the group become bogged down in the detail of these verses but note that, according to Paul, the truth about God's eternal power and divine nature is evident to everyone because of creation. Many people 'suppress the truth by their wickedness' (verse 18), meaning that habitual sin makes it easy to ignore and bury what we know in our consciences to be true about God. Paul explains this further – individuals choose not to believe the truth about God but to believe lies and worship idols. We prefer to make up our own 'gods' and worldview rather than acknowledge the true God.

6. The truth of God – the gospel, his Word in the Bible – guides us (Psalm 43:3); sets us free from sin (John 8:32); and saves us (James 1:18).

7. Because Jesus is the truth we can trust him and his Word in all circumstances. This means, for example, that we can rest in the promise of his presence and power; we can trust his sovereignty when we can't see him at work in our lives; we can believe his assurance of our home in heaven.

8. When we share the gospel we must speak the truth. That doesn't mean we bombard people with all that we know about God the first time we meet them. But it does mean that what we say to them is true; not watered-down or sugar-coated. We must also be full of grace like Christ, so though people might find offence in the gospel message they are not offended by our manner (2 Corinthians 2:15–16). Discuss how you might share the truth of the gospel with grace in these various scenarios. It may not always mean talking about the gospel but letting its power shine from our lives (1 Peter 3:1–2). It may mean offering forgiveness in a difficult situation; showing care and concern;

talking through a gospel leaflet with our children; explaining our testimony to work colleagues; or going with them to an Alpha or Christianity Explored course.

9. • **'There are many pathways to God'** – in our conversations we need to graciously point out that as each religion has its own set of beliefs, this statement simply cannot be true. If religions have different sets of beliefs, then they cannot all be true. In contrast to this pluralistic view, Christianity says Jesus is the only way to God; this is an exclusive claim that we can encourage people to investigate.

   • **'The Bible can't claim a monopoly on truth'** – it is true there have been many non-Christian scientists who have made helpful discoveries that have enriched our understanding of the world. The Bible does not claim to tell us everything about life; it doesn't give a detailed explanation of creation, or of how the world will end, for example. But the Bible offers us a framework to make sense of the world; it explains true wisdom, not just knowledge and facts. The Bible presents us with a sovereign God we can trust. He is truth, so it follows that all truth, wherever it is found, is God's truth; it belongs to him and comes from him.

   • **'Truth is what is true for me'** – this relativistic approach assumes there is no objective truth; truth is only what we feel or perceive. This argument can be countered by proving there *is* objective truth: it is true the leaves fall in autumn; the tides come in and out. If objective truth exists, surely it is worth investigating whether this applies to Christianity? Perhaps it is comfortable to make up our own belief system, but in the face of other belief systems all claiming to be true it doesn't stand up to rigorous scrutiny.

10. Walking in God's truth is essentially walking in God's ways: keeping his commandments, developing our relationship with him, living in the power of the Holy Spirit, living out his values and reflecting his character. To do this we need to be intentional about getting to know

God through his Word and in prayer; being in prayer/accountability groups where others challenge and spur us on in the faith; committing ourselves to a local church and being active in Christian service. Walking in God's truth essentially means being a disciple of Christ.

SESSION 2

Real identity

1. This issue is important because our identity helps us know where we fit in the world; it gives us a sense of belonging and value. How other people identify us reveals what they think of us.

2. Paul describes us as 'brothers and sisters' of other believers (verse 12), 'children of God' (verse 14), 'God's children' (verse 16), 'heirs of God and co-heirs with Christ' (verse 17). These titles base our new identity in belonging to God and other believers.

3. We received this new identity of being 'in Christ' not through our own accomplishments, but because of Christ's death on the cross. Jesus was the sin offering; he took our place on the cross, and the requirements of the law were fully met by his sacrifice. The Holy Spirit sets us free from death and the power of sin so we are free to obey God.

4. The Holy Spirit – the same Spirit who raised Jesus from the dead – living in a person, helping them fight sin and be obedient to Christ is the hallmark of a believer. The Spirit is also a guarantee of our future bodily resurrection.

5. The Holy Spirit helps us 'put to death' sinful behaviour. This means God's Spirit gives us strength to say 'no' to sin and resist temptation; he helps us deny ourselves in order to obey God's will. Verse 14 says the Holy Spirit 'leads us' – he guides us in ways which please God, he reminds us of God's truth, and he helps us in our pursuit of holiness. The Holy Spirit confirms to us that we're God's children, so we no longer need to live in fear of God's condemnation for our sins.

6. Peter uses various images to describe the church: a temple made of individual living stones, a holy and royal priesthood, a holy nation, a chosen people, and a people belonging to God. The picture of the stones reminds us that the church derives its life and identity from Christ. We are his and he is the living Stone, the cornerstone. It's not just individuals who have the Holy Spirit – the church as a body is

indwelt with God's Spirit. Calling believers 'holy priests' reflects the high calling we have to reflect the holiness of God, to be set apart for his service. As priests our role is to offer sacrifices – the sacrifice of our lives to God. The church is called to be a group of people who praise God, not just in songs but in the way we live and minister in our community. The other titles in the list remind us that we are called by God, chosen by him, precious and loved by him.

7. Our new identity means that we are 'foreigners and exiles' (verse 11). We have different values from our contemporaries, and our behaviour must reflect that our true home and citizenship is in heaven. In the Holy Spirit's power we must avoid sin, even though it entices us. We will have to wrestle with sin, avoid temptation and in its place pursue holiness. God wants us to do good and live such winsome lives that unbelievers are influenced to follow our example and turn to him.

8. If the Holy Spirit is going to lead us, we need to listen to him speak through the Bible and in prayer. We become deaf to his promptings if we regularly disobey him and disregard his voice. But if through his strength we strive to become more holy, avoiding sin and actively denying it room in our lives, then we become more in tune to his promptings (Romans 8:15). Sometimes periods of fasting, corporate prayer and asking the advice of a mature believer can help us discern where the Holy Spirit is leading.

9. We need to be sensitive when talking to unbelievers about this issue. But we can explain that if it was merely our own assertion that we are God's children and have a home in heaven, then yes, we would be arrogant. But the point Paul makes in Romans is that it is God who declares us his children; it is the Holy Spirit who gives us the confidence to be sure it is true. Pray that our friends would see the Holy Spirit's work in our lives. If they can see the reality of this, then they may accept the rest of the truth of Christianity and accept Jesus as their Saviour.

10. As Christians we don't just have an individual identity; we have a collective identity – we are part of God's family, the church. So we

need to recognize that fellow believers are our brothers and sisters and that all the love God has for us he has for each one of them. Being part of small groups and ministry teams helps us grow in holiness as we learn to bear others' burdens, use our spiritual gifts, witness and serve in the community. Discussions in our Bible study groups or conversations with Christian friends may challenge us about our sin, hold us accountable for spiritual transformation, or renew our strength to face temptation. Being part of larger church services where the Bible is taught and we respond in collective worship helps us keep our focus on Christ and living for him. All of these are means God uses to remind us of our real individual and corporate identity as children of God.

SESSION 3

Real wisdom

1. We have all met people who possess factual knowledge but no wisdom whatsoever. Wisdom is more than knowledge; it is knowing what to do with the facts and how to relate to others. It is also being able to handle the unpredictability of life with resourcefulness and calmness, and to learn from our experiences. Referring to Job 28 David Atkinson writes, 'Human wisdom is demonstrated in an ability to cope – to cope with the ordinary demands of day-to-day morality; to cope with knowing what to do, how to govern, how to rule; to cope with the raw materials of the craftsmen's skills' (Atkinson, *The Message of Job*, p. 119).

2a. The search for wisdom is worthwhile because it is so valuable – it is priceless. Gold and precious stones cannot buy it. All the treasures of the world combined would not be enough to purchase it.

2b. Wisdom cannot be found in this world. It's hidden from humans; even birds with their higher vantage point in the sky cannot find it. Even if we could go down to the depths of the seas (places associated with the dead), we could not find wisdom.

3. Only God knows the way to wisdom because only he can see everything under the heavens. Wisdom is the centrepiece of God's creation of the universe; when he was ordering the weather systems, he established and tested wisdom.

4. We can access wisdom by 'fearing the Lord'. Only God can open the way of wisdom to us. But notice wisdom is not finding the answer to all our questions; wisdom is trusting in God, the one who alone knows all the answers.

5. In this example Abraham is a model of what it means to 'fear God'. He took God at his word. Isaac was the child of the promise, through whom Abraham was supposed to have many descendants; killing him would apparently thwart all these plans. But Abraham trusted that God would fulfil his promise, even though he wasn't sure how.

Abraham was willing to sacrifice his precious, much-loved son to be obedient to God. Submitting our wills to God, even when we can't see the big picture and don't understand what God is doing, is what it means to 'fear God'. (Try not to let the group wander off track – 'fearing God' never means murder or child sacrifice!)

6. • **Psalm 147:11** – 'fearing God' means putting our hope, our trust, in God's character. We trust his unfailing love – which encapsulates his mercy, grace and faithfulness – especially when we cannot see his hand at work in the difficult circumstances of our lives.

   • **Proverbs 8:13** – 'fearing the Lord' means to 'hate evil'. This means avoiding sin, not putting ourselves in the way of temptation, and taking drastic measures to tackle the sin in our lives. Positively, it means pursuing righteous thoughts and behaviour.

   • **Isaiah 33:6** – 'fearing the Lord' is the way to access all the treasures in Christ. When we 'fear him', Christ becomes our rock and security, he saves us, and brings us God's wisdom and knowledge.

7a. According to Psalm 1:1–2, we are blessed by God when we live wisely, revering and obeying him. Wise living means building our life on God's work, rather than joining in with those who do evil and who mock God. This does not mean avoiding non-Christians, but it does mean we don't get involved with their sinful behaviour. It means digging deep into God's Word – letting it penetrate and feed our soul on a daily basis.

7b. When we live wisely, nourishing our souls on God's Word, then we are spiritually fruitful – we grow in Christ-like characteristics. With our roots deeply embedded in God and his Word, we have a stability, peace and security which is not dependent on life's circumstances.

8. If we want new believers (of whatever age) to grow as disciples and live wisely, we need to give them some help. We can show them how to read the Bible. For example, explain how to start your Bible reading

with prayer, look at the context, discover what we learn about God from the passage and apply the lessons personally. We also need to model spiritual maturity for new believers, perhaps developing a mentoring relationship or involving them in Christian service with us. Encourage them to be part of a prayer/accountability group where there is honest discussion about how God's Word applies to life. Provide them with good books and Bible study resources. There are lots of ways to encourage new believers. Don't overwhelm them, but pray God would show you how best to help them.

9. When we suffer, we often look for reasons – have I done something wrong, am I being punished for past sin? We question God's love and his justice in allowing us to suffer when so many others do not. Focusing on God's wisdom takes us out of the realm of justice we understand – where the world needs to make sense, where we have to have logical reasons, where we feel in control – and it transports us to God's throne where he controls the whole cosmos, where he is dealing with situations we cannot comprehend. Focusing on God's wisdom allows us leave our questions with him, to trust that he knows best and is working for his glory in the world, that our suffering is part of that.

10. Share with each other as it is appropriate. Sometimes it is difficult to resist our desire to be in charge and control things. Perhaps when it comes to our children or our career we find it hard to trust God; we would much rather engineer situations ourselves. Discuss practical ways we can learn to trust God's wisdom, perhaps praying about particular circumstances, and meditating on verses about God's wisdom to remind ourselves he is ultimately in charge and trustworthy. Often our submission to God in these areas is something we need to do again and again.

SESSION 4

Real purpose

1. We often feel a sense of purpose and satisfaction from doing our job well, from being a parent, or putting our skills and talents to good use. God designed us this way (Genesis 1:28–30). The aim of this study is to affirm these roles and responsibilities but to also see the overarching purpose of our lives – to know Christ and make him known – and explore how we make this a reality.

2. 'Knowing Christ' does not refer to a factual knowledge but means to experience God and enjoy a union with Christ which is possible because of his work on the cross. 'Knowing Christ' is about a continuing, growing relationship with God. It means to experience and rely on the Holy Spirit's power in our lives, the same power which raised Jesus from the dead. It also means sharing the suffering of Christ, suffering for God's sake.

3. Paul realized that his past achievements counted for nothing; he understood that everything which had previously given him purpose and significance was worthless. The turning point was acknowledging that his restored relationship with God was not based on his achievements but on trusting in God's righteousness. Only God could justify him, and only following and serving him could give his life purpose and meaning.

4. Paul imagines himself as a runner in a race and uses phrases like 'pressing on', 'forgetting what is behind' and 'straining forward'. He describes the ruthless focus of a runner who ignores all other distractions so that he can win the goal – heavenly glory with Christ.

5. • **Suffering** – Paul viewed his suffering as worthwhile because it meant that he could preach the gospel to the guards who were chained to him in prison and because it motivated others to preach the gospel. His sufferings were secondary to spreading the gospel.

- **Death** – wanting to know Christ was Paul's driving ambition and purpose. He didn't really mind if he lived or died because his life found its meaning in Christ, and death meant he would be with Christ.

- **Ministry** – Paul wasn't satisfied to know Christ himself; he wanted to make Christ known to others. He was eager for the Philippians to make progress in their faith and for the gospel to be the driving force in their lives.

6. God's purpose is that we would do the good works that he planned in advance for us to do (Ephesians 2:10), we would live holy lives (2 Timothy 1:9), and we would share the gospel with others (2 Corinthians 5:18–20).

7. We need to forget about our sinful past, in the sense that we acknowledge Christ's death on the cross has paid the punishment for our sin and made us right with God. We are not to be held back by feelings of guilt or shame. Neither should we depend on memories of past good times with God. Our knowledge and experience of God should be growing each day as we come before him for fresh grace and mercy.

   We can easily become distracted from 'pressing on' in our relationship with God by busyness, self-centredness, suffering, bitterness, and countless other things. 'Straining forwards' means we remove these distractions, we don't give in to lethargy in our devotional lives, we discipline ourselves towards spiritual transformation through, for example, Bible reading, prayer and Christian fellowship.

8. Encourage each other to 'make Christ known' in your sphere of influence by praying for non-Christian friends, inviting them to an Alpha course, sharing your life with them so they can see your different purpose and values up close. Discuss together how best to share the gospel in your community – what has worked and what hasn't? Be honest that although not all of us are natural evangelists we are all Christ's ambassadors and are charged with representing him.

9. Sometimes the relentless monotony of work or parenting can make our daily tasks seem purposeless; it is hard to see their eternal significance. But praying through our day, learning to be conscious of God's presence, changing our attitude so that we want to serve him, seeing difficulties as opportunities to trust God and allowing him to work in our lives, all help us live for God's glory and not our own. When we are doing our work or parenting for God's pleasure and glory, seeking to promote his values, then what we are doing takes on eternal significance.

10. Encourage the group to see that our real purpose in life is to 'know Christ and make him known', but we do this in the individual context God has placed us in – our work, family and community. We all have the same main purpose, but how we work it out will be unique for each person.

Real security

1. There are many ways people try to make themselves feel secure. For example, they may work hard to achieve financial security; go to the gym and buy nice clothes so they feel secure about their body image; or invest in a good education to secure their children's future.

2. This psalm doesn't give any evidence that life is easier for those who trust in Christ. In verses 1–3 the psalmist mentions physical threats such as earthquakes, floods and storms. The effect is so great it seems as if the earth is breaking up and sinking beneath the seas. And verses 6 and 9 mention political upheaval and war. Christians face the same troubles and suffering as non-Christians do. The difference, as Psalm 46 explains, is that God promises his protection, strength and ever-present help, so there is no need to fear as we go through difficult times. His power and presence are more than a match for any of life's emergencies. He also promises his people joy in the darkness (verse 4) and deliverance (verse 5).

3. God's security is for those who take their refuge in him (verse 1) and acknowledge him as God (verse 10). Others will one day be forced to acknowledge God's sovereign control over the earth (verses 6, 10) but they will face judgement for their unbelief (verses 8–9).

4. Verse 10 points forward to the day when God's sovereignty will be displayed throughout the earth and everyone will exalt him. On this day, when Christ returns, the significance of Jesus' death, resurrection and ascension will be evident to all. In the meantime, although we suffer, we look forward to that final day, knowing our victory and salvation are secure because of all that Christ accomplished on the cross.

5. • **Romans 8:28** – we can be certain that our earthly struggles have a redemptive value. The 'good' that God works all things together for is to make us more like Jesus.

- **Philippians 1:4–6** – whatever struggles we face, we can be secure in the knowledge that God will not give up on us. One day our salvation will be complete, and we will be like Christ.

- **Hebrews 4:14–16** – we can be secure in our faith and boldly approach God, knowing that Jesus is our High Priest who is always interceding for us, understanding our struggles and presenting us before God.

6.
- **John 10:27–30** – our eternal security is in Christ's hand and in the Father's hand. In a sense, it is doubly secure. Like a good shepherd, Jesus protects each one of his sheep. Jesus promises those who are his will 'never perish.'

- **Romans 5:6–11** – Christ died for us while we were still sinners, when we had done nothing good or worthy. Our salvation does not depend on anything we have done or could do; it depends entirely on God's grace in sending Jesus to die in our place. Because Jesus paid for our sin on the cross, our salvation is secure and our relationship with God is restored. And even now, the risen Jesus lives to intercede for us.

- **Romans 8:35–39** – struggles, hardship and suffering do not mean our salvation is in doubt; these elements have always been part of the Christian life. Indeed even in the midst of hardships we are assured of God's love, our union with him and our ultimate salvation.

7. The psalmist recalled all the mighty acts he had seen and heard about God doing. He reflected on specific events like the Israelites' deliverance from Egypt, the crossing of the Red Sea, and God guiding his people in the wilderness. At a time when God seemed inactive and the psalmist wrestled with doubts about God's love, he meditated on these truths (verse 12) to remind himself of God's faithfulness and power.

8. Discuss honestly the doubts and struggles that have challenged your faith; the specific ways your faith was renewed during these times; and

how these occasions have been an opportunity to witness to believers and unbelievers about God's faithfulness.

9. Consider the local and national challenges the church faces, such as: the debate surrounding human sexuality; the increase in secularism; the prevalence of relativism; and concern surrounding issues related to the beginning and end of life. In the face of these challenges how can the church remain secure? Discuss factors such as renewing our confidence in the authority of the Bible; studying historical/apologetic material and engaging in dialogue with others; and showing pastoral care and kindness to those in our communities struggling with these issues.

10. We can see where our trust is placed by the way we spend our money, the things we invest our time and energies in, and the behaviour we cultivate. So look at your direct debits – do these show you are investing in God's kingdom or simply securing your financial future? Reflect back on your conversations and priorities last week – do they show you are trusting in God's wisdom, goodness and sovereignty? Do your behaviour and attitudes show you are living for God's reward or trying to impress others? When you pray, do you trust God to answer according to his will, or do you seek to engineer circumstances yourself? Discuss all these issues as honestly as you can and come up with practical changes you can make to indicate your security is in God alone.

SESSION 6

Real treasure

1. We all have different priorities, and sometimes others can see what we value more clearly than we can. Perhaps we treasure our families, careers, reputation, holidays, bodies or athletic abilities. It's not wrong to enjoy any of these things, but this study will help us think through the priorities God wants us to have and make sure we treasure him above all else.

2. The first man just happened upon the treasure as he was working in the field. In contrast, the merchant was searching diligently for the fine pearl. In the same way, some people find God as if by accident, while others find him after a careful search, perhaps even after trying other faiths.

3. The first man seems to have been a farm labourer, a poor man who was working in someone else's field. The second was a rich businessman. Heaven will be made up of all sorts of people from a variety of backgrounds.

4. Both these parables stress the tremendous worth of the kingdom of heaven and that we have to let go of everything else in order to obtain it.

5. • **Matthew 19:16–21** – an authentic relationship with God does not just involve keeping the Ten Commandments. It means making Jesus your greatest passion and highest priority. The rich young man was told to give away his wealth, not because you need to be poor to become a Christian, but because his wealth stood in the way of loving God wholeheartedly.

    • **John 12:23–26** – to find real treasure, one must be willing to follow Christ's example and sacrifice personal ambition, success and self-centredness to follow God's will and priorities. The spiritual world imitates the natural world of seeds and plants – life comes through death.

- **1 Timothy 6:17–19** – to gain eternal life and to enjoy satisfaction in God we must trust him rather than any worldly wealth. This new perspective is evidenced by our willingness to share, our good deeds and our humble attitude.

6. We can never out-give God. Matthew 19:29–30 promises that we will be recompensed for any sacrifices we have made and will receive eternal life.

7. When we become Christians, Christ comes to live inside us by the power of the Holy Spirit. Paul likens it to keeping treasure in the cracked and broken clay jars used for carrying water every day. Our lives are the jars – broken, fragile, ordinary – from which God's power and glory shine. Like a jeweller's black cloth on which diamonds are displayed, our lives are the background from which God's glory shines.

8. It seems strange, but even in church there is the possibility of sidelining Christ. We can get so busy with ministry, impacting our communities and planning church services that we lose Christ as our focal point and reason for being. Consider your own church context: how can you keep Christ as your priority? Some ideas could include making sure our worship times are Christ-focused, our preaching is based on the Bible, and our prayers are filled with adoration and are not just a shopping list. Those of us who are not church leaders may feel we cannot influence church culture, but do not underestimate the difference your passionate devotional life can have on other believers.

9. We know that our financial giving to God should be considered and regular (2 Corinthians 9:7) and God wants us to surrender ourselves to him daily (Romans 12:1). However, perhaps like Mary, we could give God a love gift – an extravagant, costly gift to show him how much we love him. Pray God will show you what that gift could be.

10. As we go through struggles and suffering and are aware of our frailty and brokenness, it is encouraging to remember that Christ is in us. The Holy Spirit in us is a promise that glory will one day be ours and

in the meantime we can rely on his strength and grace. This image of the broken jar reminds us our struggles can have value – our brokenness can let the light of Christ shine out even more. God can even use our difficulties to point people to himself.

Real hope

1. We hope for many things in life. For example, we may hope to progress in our careers; that our home sells so we can buy a bigger one; that our children stay healthy and make wise choices. This study will help us see that hope in Christ impacts our lives now and for eternity, regardless of how our other ambitions turn out.

2. We are waiting for God's glory to be fully revealed in us when Jesus comes again. On that day our redemption will be complete; we will receive our full inheritance as believers. We will be seen for what we really are – the children of God. Having the full weight of God's glory in us will make our present sufferings pale into insignificance. And it's not only believers eagerly waiting for this final day. Romans 8:19–22 reminds us that the whole of creation is longing for restoration and renewal, an end to death and decay.

3. Firstly, the measure of the Holy Spirit we have now is like a down payment, a promise that one day full transformation will happen. Secondly, God has promised that he will finish the process he has started – becoming a Christian is the first part in God's plan to make us more like his Son which ends in our glorification.

4. Whatever struggles we may be facing, we can have hope in God because we know that he is *for* us. We have been justified – Christ's work on the cross means that Satan can no longer accuse us. Our sin has been paid for. Jesus is now constantly interceding for us before God, pleading our case. We can have security, joy and peace, knowing that we are loved by God. Our struggles do not mean that God has stopped loving us: in fact, the opposite is true. God never stops working for our good, wanting to conform us into the image of Christ.

5. Jesus' resurrection is the proof that we will also be raised from the dead, full salvation will come and one day we will receive our eternal

inheritance in heaven. This inheritance, all the good things we will receive from our heavenly Father, cannot be spoiled or lost. Until that final day, God promises that his power is guarding our faith, keeping us faithful.

6. • **1 Peter 1:6–7** reminds us that God does not waste difficult times; they can be used by him to refine and prove our faith.

   • **2 Corinthians 4:16–18** encourages us that Jesus renews us; that spiritual transformation can happen during our darkest days. Our hardships are only temporary compared to the eternal glory of God we will share.

7. • **Isaiah 40:31** – as we put our hope and trust in God, he promises to renew our strength.

   • **1 Thessalonians 1:3** – hope helps us to endure through hardships.

   • **Hebrews 6:17–20** – Christian hope is like an anchor for our soul; because it is based on heavenly realities it gives us stability and security.

   • **1 John 3:3** – hope in God motivates us to purify ourselves, to live holy lives so that we are ready for Christ's return.

8. • Our **Christian friends** probably know what the Bible says about putting their hope in God in difficult times. It is often not helpful to quote Bible verses: instead, listen, pray with them and for them, and offer any practical help you can. If you can, encourage them to keep their focus on God and keep trusting in him.

   • Our **non-Christian friends** don't share our beliefs but they watch our behaviour, listen to our conversations, and see our priorities and values lived out. We can share our hope in God with them by living with God at the centre, trusting him in difficult times, thanking him in the good times, sharing about God when opportunities arise, giving practical help and care when our friends are in need.

- In **our communities** there are lots of opportunities to do good, to care for the poor, to support those in need, to live out God's values and share his message of hope in practical ways.

9. Discuss how these Bible verses challenge and comfort you in difficult times. Perhaps you need the challenge of remembering that God wants to use your suffering to refine your faith, to make you more like Christ. Perhaps reminding yourself about the eternal realities of heaven and of our future hope is a comfort during difficult times.

10. We all have aspirations for ourselves and our families, but use this study to remind the group of the very real, secure hope of heaven and eternal realities that we have. And even in life's difficulties we have the daily hope of Christ's presence and the knowledge that he is acting in all the circumstances of our lives. Discuss practical ways to keep this real hope your main focus.

Bibliography

Ash, Christopher, *Out of the Storm: Grappling with God in the Book of Job* (IVP, 2004)

Atkinson, David, *The Message of Job* (IVP, 1991)

Carson, Don, *The Gospel According to John* (IVP, 1991)

Elliot, Elisabeth, *In the Shadow of the Almighty* (Harper and Row, 1958)

Ellsworth, Roger, *Opening up Philippians* (Day One Publications, 2004)

Grudem, Wayne, *Systematic Theology* (IVP/Zondervan, 1994)

Keller, Timothy, *Galatians for You* (The Good Book Company, 2013)

Lewis, C. S., 'Is Theology Poetry?', in *C.S. Lewis: Essay Collection* (Collins, 2001)

Mallard, Paul, *Invest Your Suffering* (IVP, 2013)

McGrath, Alister, *Doubt in Perspective* (IVP, 2006)

McGrath, Alister, *Mere Theology* (SPCK, 2010)

Mounce, Robert, *New International Biblical Commentary: Matthew* (Hendrickson/Paternoster Press, 1995)

Packer, J. I., *Knowing God* (Hodder and Stoughton, 1973)

Roseveare, Helen, in *Word to the World* (Authentic, 2011)

Sinkinson, Chris, *Confident Christianity* (IVP, 2012)

Walton, John, *Job: The New International Commentary* (Zondervan, 2012)

About Keswick Ministries

The vision of *Keswick Ministries* is *the spiritual renewal of God's people for his mission in today's world.*

We are committed to the deepening of the spiritual life in individuals and church communities through the careful exposition and application of Scripture, with the following priorities:

- **Lordship of Christ**: to encourage submission to the Lordship of Christ in all areas of personal and corporate living.

- **Transformation by Word and Spirit**: to encourage active obedience to God's Word through a dependency upon the indwelling and fullness of the Holy Spirit for life-transformation and effective living.

- **Evangelism and mission**: to provoke a strong commitment to evangelism and mission in the UK and worldwide.

- **Whole-life discipleship**: to stimulate the discipling and training of people of all ages in godliness, service and sacrificial living, equipping them to participate in the mission of God in every area of life.

- **Unity and family**: to provide a practical demonstration of evangelical unity across denominations and across generations.

Keswick Ministries seeks to achieve its aims by:

- sustaining and developing the three-week summer Convention in Keswick UK, teaching and training Christians of all ages and backgrounds;

- providing training for preachers, leaders and youth and children's workers in different parts of the UK;

- strengthening the network of 'Keswick' events in towns and cities around the UK;

- producing and promoting resources (books, DVDs and downloads, as well as TV and radio programmes) so that Keswick's teaching ministry is brought to a wider audience around the world;

- providing a year-round residential centre in Keswick for the use of church groups and Christian organisations;

- encouraging an international movement by building relationships with the many 'Keswicks' around the world, thereby seeking to strengthen local churches in their life and mission.

For **further information**, please see our website:
www.keswickministries.org
or contact our office:

Email: info@keswickministries.org
Tel: 017687 80075
Mail: Keswick Ministries, Convention Centre, Skiddaw Street,
Keswick CA12 4BY, England.

THE WHOLE OF LIFE
for CHRIST

WEEK 1	**11–17 JULY**	John Risbridger
WEEK 2	**18–24 JULY**	Paul Mallard
WEEK 3	**25–31 JULY**	Liam Goligher

VISIT WWW.KESWICKMINISTRIES.ORG

2015
THE KESWICK CONVENTION
Keswick ministries

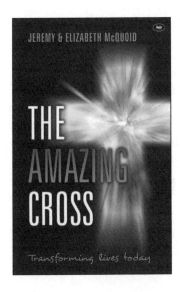

also by Elizabeth McQuoid

The Amazing Cross
Transforming lives today
Jeremy & Elizabeth McQuoid

ISBN: 978-1-84474-587-6
192 pages, paperback

The cross of Christ is the heartbeat of Christianity. It is a place of pain and horror, wonder and beauty, all at the same time. It is the place where our sin collided gloriously with God's grace.

But do we really understand what the cross is all about? Or are we so caught up in the peripherals of the faith that we have forgotten the core? We need to ask ourselves:

• How deep an impact has the cross made on my personality?
• Do I live in the light of the freedom it has won for me?
• Am I dying to myself every day, so that I can live for Christ?
• Do I face suffering with faith and assurance?
• Can I face death in the light of the hope of the resurrection?

The authors present us with a contemporary challenge to place all of our lives, every thought, word and deed, under the shadow of the amazing cross, and allow that cross to transform us here and now.

'It is an ideal introduction to the heart of the Christian gospel, and a very welcome addition to the Keswick Foundation series.' Jonathan Lamb

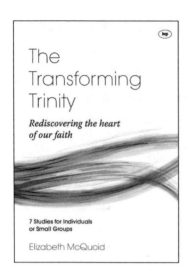

also by Elizabeth McQuoid

KESWICK STUDY GUIDE

The Transforming Trinity

Rediscovering the heart of our faith
Elizabeth McQuoid

ISBN: 978-1-84474-906-5
80 pages, booklet

Does believing in the Trinity make any difference in real life?

These seven studies will help you grow in your understanding of the inexhaustible riches of the Trinity. Find out why the Trinity is central to our beliefs and fundamental to the working out of our faith.

Learn to worship the triune God more fully, reflect his image more clearly, and experience his transforming power in your life. Learn what it really means to know the Father, follow the Son, and walk in the Spirit.

Because the Trinity is at the heart of Christian faith and life.

'Encounter and be transformed by the living God, Father, Son and Spirit. Highly recommended!' Dr Steve Brady

'Will help you explore this wonderful theme, engaging your heart, stretching your mind and changing your life!' John Risbridger

'A feast for individuals and Bible study groups.' Sam Allberry

Available from your local Christian bookshop or **www.thinkivp.com**